NICK FAWCETT

Stop

&

Stare

A reflective
Lent course

kevin
mayhew

First published in 2007 by

KEVIN MAYHEW LTD
Buxhall, Stowmarket, Suffolk, IP14 3BW
E-mail: info@kevinmayhew.com
www.kevinmayhew.com

Acknowledgements:
Page 5 – 'Leisure' by William Henry Davies – the
Trustees to the estate of William Henry Davies
Page 44 – Prayer by Evelyn Underhill – the Evelyn
Underhill Association
Page 51 – 'God's World' by Edna St Vincent Millay
– the Successors to Edna St Vincent Millay
Page 58 – Poem by Patience Strong – the Estate of
Patience Strong

9 8 7 6 5 4 3 2 1 0

ISBN 978 1 84417 839 1
Catalogue No. 1501050

Cover design by Sara-Jane Came
Edited and typeset by Katherine Laidler

Printed and bound in Great Britain

Contents

What is this life if, full of care,
we have no time to stand and stare? –
No time to stand beneath the boughs,
and stare as long as sheep and cows:
no time to see, when woods we pass,
where squirrels hide their nuts in grass:
no time to see, in broad daylight,
streams full of stars, like skies at night:
no time to turn at Beauty's glance,
and watch her feet, how they can dance:
no time to wait till her mouth can
enrich that smile her eyes began?
A poor life this if, full of care,
we have no time to stand and stare.

'Leisure' by William Henry Davies (1871–1940)

Dedicated to the members and clergy of

Trinity Methodist and United Reformed Church, Cheadle
St Chad's Roman Catholic Church, Cheadle
St James' Parish Church, Gatley
and Gatley United Reformed Church . . .

with thanks for your generous words of encouragement

Introduction

What are you doing for Lent? Traditionally this is a season for sacrifice and self-denial, exemplified by the idea of 'giving something up for Lent'. For some that may mean denying themselves certain treats or luxuries, giving the money saved to a good cause. Others focus on conquering a vice or weakness, Lent being seen as the ideal opportunity to put this behind them once and for all. There's another equally important way of observing this season, however, and that's through making it a time for quiet reflection. In our modern world, opportunities for contemplation are often sadly lacking, tending to be crowded out of our lives. Why this should be, what effect it has, and the riches we miss as a result are the subject of this book. I've based it on words that have captured the hearts of generations: the celebrated poem 'What is this life?' by William Henry Davies.

Why has this poem struck such a chord? Partly, of course, it's the beauty of the poet's language and the images he conjures up, but equally important perhaps is that he reminds us of something fundamental to life which we're uncomfortably conscious of having lost: that vital ability to stop and stare. We had it once in the relatively carefree days of childhood, but little by little the demands of daily life have pushed it to the sidelines, relegating it to the periphery of our lives.

The thrust of Davies' poem is, of course, the natural world, but for Christians it goes beyond that, speaking of the need to reflect also on the things of God. Not that the two are mutually exclusive, for spiritual realities are often only glimpsed when we pause in the press of a busy day to take stock, allowing the ordinary to become special, the secular sacred, the commonplace touched by the divine. But this ability to reflect can be obscured by the weight of daily care in a host of guises, so it's here that I begin, exploring what such cares might be and how best we can face them. Most pressing a concern for many is the pressure of time, real or imagined, so it's to this I turn next, asking whether we see it as an obstacle or opportunity, as something positive to be welcomed or negative to be feared. Our third session takes us to the heart of Davies' poem, exploring the wonder of nature and the countless ways it can not only move and inspire but also speak of God. From here we move in the next session to consider how almost every part of life, even the most ordinary and familiar, can point to God if we're only ready to pause and ponder. Session five draws things together, emphasising the need to stop and stare not just during Lent but always.

Given the subject matter, I've avoided making this a study book, my aim instead being to provide a tool for reflection. In each session, after an opening prayer, introduction, readings and points for discussion, I offer a mixture of poems, prayers, proverbs and other material (drawn from my own books and others) designed to stimulate quiet contemplation. You may find it helpful, weather permitting, to go outside and find a quiet spot in which to read and reflect. Between each reading I've left time for silence. Don't skip these – they are as important as any of the words, if not more so, affording the opportunity to stop and stare in practice.

I know from experience how easy it is to get sucked into the vortex of perpetual activity, believing we have no time to stand and stare. Writing this book has arisen from that realisation and has provided a valuable lesson. It is my hope that something in these pages may speak to you in turn so that this Lent may become the gateway to a more reflective life and faith.

NICK FAWCETT

Session 1
Full of care?

What is this life if, full of care,

we have no time to stand and stare?

Aim

To reflect on the pressures, cares and responsibilities life brings, and to consider them in the light of Christ.

Introductory verse

The man's very words are these: 'I am worn out, O God, fit to drop. How can I hope to get through?' (Proverbs 30:1)

Prayer

Lord,
  we come with our faults,
  our weaknesses
  and our lack of faith,
  seeking your mercy
  and your renewing touch.
Speak to us here.
Meet with us everywhere.

We come with our cares –
    the pressures we face each day,
    the problems we wrestle with,
    the burdens we carry and long to put down,
    seeking your help to bear them
    and to let go of what we can.
Speak to us here.
Meet with us everywhere.

We come with our hurts,
    our pain,
    our sorrow
    and our fears,
    seeking strength in times of adversity
    and the healing touch of your hand.
Speak to us here.
Meet with us everywhere.

We come together,
    looking for guidance, nurture and inspiration,
    seeking above all a deeper faith
    and fuller knowledge of you.
Speak to us here.
Meet with us everywhere.
Amen.

Introduction

'Full of care' – does that describe you? Strangely, if there's one malaise that could be said to characterise modern-day Western society, it's probably exactly this, as testified to all too eloquently by the waiting lists of numerous GPs, psychiatrists, counsellors and other therapists. We seem to be burdened as never before by pressures, worries, fears and phobias, countless people being close to buckling under the strain of it all. Most, though, are under-standably reluctant to admit it. After all, we in the West are the lucky ones, fortunate enough to have a standard of living that most of the world's population can only dream of. What right have we to feel troubled or careworn? Surely we should be thankful for our lot, greeting each day with celebration rather than anxiety, and rejoicing in our plenty? There's undeniably truth in such an argument, few of us having any idea of what it means to suffer real hardship, yet, for all that, the prosperity and material comforts many of us enjoy have been bought at a price: the price of inner tranquillity and contentment.

Just why that is and what we can do about it is the subject of this book, and will be explored in more detail in subsequent sessions, but here I want to consider further the nature of our cares, asking how best we should approach them. Some may be specific, including, for example, broken relationships, bereavement, health worries or financial insecurity; others may be harder to pin down, ranging from a sense of insecurity to phobias to depression; others again may 'merely' be the weight of life's daily demands and responsibilities – a sense that there's always something to be done, a schedule to fulfil, a deadline to meet. More likely, we find ourselves facing a combination of these, wrestling, as it were, on several fronts.

So how do we respond to such troubles? A typical approach is to indulge in frantic activity, almost as though through keeping busy we can keep our cares at bay. Don't stop, we tell ourselves, or that problem will catch up with us and drag us down. Stay occupied, get our head down, and we'll somehow muddle through. For others the response is very different. They feel paralysed by their worries, increasingly unable to face anything, so they turn in on themselves, retreating ever deeper into their lonely private world. Either way, cares build up until they exert an unremitting stranglehold, squeezing the joy out of life until there seems little left worth living for. I've seen it happen all too often, fears and anxieties stealthily taking over until each day is lived under their shadow and all else is obscured.

11

So what else might we try? A possibility that may surprise you is suggested to me by the well-loved hymn of Johnson Oatman, 'Count your blessings'. That, of course, is excellent advice in itself, for simply listing our reasons to be cheerful can go a long way in helping us see past our problems. But I'm thinking here along different lines: of counting our *cares*. That too can be useful, not with a view to morbid introspection but simply as a way of getting things into perspective. Objectively identifying our troubles can help us face them, for we see each then for what it is, rather than allowing them en masse to become a nebulous dark cloud that hangs menacingly over life.

With our cares, however, we don't just need to 'count them one by one'; we need also to *tackle* them one at a time. It's impossible to overstate how important that is. None of us can do everything at once, and the more we try to juggle, the more likely we are to make a hash of things. Don't try to put everything right in a day; face your problems one by one, and let that be enough.

That's essentially what Jesus said in the Sermon on the Mount. 'Do not fret about tomorrow, for tomorrow will take care of itself. Let the problems of one day be sufficient for themselves' (Matthew 6:34). And that's just one of many passages we could turn to that promise help or hope to those wrestling under a weight of care; that remind us he cares about our welfare, shares our sorrows and bears our pain.

Do we have more troubles today than in times past? No. We have only to pause and consider what people have endured across the years, and what millions still endure, to realise how fortunate we are in countless ways. But that's not to say life doesn't bring its trials, for of course it does. None of us are immune from sickness, suffering, trauma or tragedy, and some experience those more than others. Faith doesn't downplay such trials for a moment. Rather it offers God's promise of strength and support, the assurance that whatever we're called to face he will see us through it. But it calls us also to consider our cares in a new light, asking whether they're all as real as they seem. 'Do not be anxious, saying, "What

12

will we eat?" or "What will we drink?" or "What will we wear?" But seek first the kingdom and righteousness of God, and you shall be given all of these in addition' (Matthew 6:31, 33). In other words, don't fret about what's unimportant – the trivia that we daily magnify out of all proportion. Don't get sucked into the rat-race, the endless cycle of wanting ever more, of climbing the ladder, of keeping up with the Joneses. Focus on what truly satisfies, on what God daily provides, and many of our troubles will suddenly melt away. Take that thought with you into the coming week, and live each day in that perspective, for as the poet rightly says, 'What is this life if, full of care, we have no time to stand and stare?'

Readings

Reflect quietly on the following, considering your cares and troubles in the light of them.

- All who are tired of carrying heavy loads, come to me and I will grant you rest. Take my yoke on you and learn from me, for I am tender and unassuming in heart, and you will find rest for your souls – for my yoke is easy, and my burden is light. (Matthew 11:28-30)

- Do not be anxious, saying, 'What will we eat?' or 'What will we drink?' or 'What will we wear?' But seek first the kingdom and righteousness of God, and you shall be given all of these in addition. Which of you by worrying can add one cubit to your stature? Therefore do not fret about tomorrow, for tomorrow will take care of itself. Let the problems of one day be sufficient. (Matthew 6:31a, 33, 34)

- Do not brood over anything, but thankfully acquaint God with all your needs through your prayers and petitions. (Philippians 4:6)

- Why is my soul disheartened and my spirit troubled within me? I put my hope in you, O God, for I will again praise you, my help and my God. (Psalm 42:5, 6a)

- My legacy to you is peace: that's what I'm giving to you, unlike anything the world can give. So, then, don't allow your heart to be anxious; have no fear. (John 14:27)

- I will lie down and sleep in peace; for you alone, O Lord, make me lie down in safety. (Psalm 4:8)

- Humble yourselves under the mighty hand of God so that, in due course, he may exalt you. Cast all your worries upon him, for he cares for you. (1 Peter 5:6, 7)

- In times of trouble he will keep me safe beneath his roof; he will hide me in the shelter of his tent and set me high upon a rock. (Psalm 27:5)

Discuss

- What practical advice does Jesus give here? How can we put it into practice? What grounds does he offer for letting go of our worries?

- What cares feature or have featured most prominently in your life? What worries do you find hardest to live with? How do you tackle these and with what degree of success?

- Do you feel guilty sometimes about feeling anxious or troubled? Why? What do you think Jesus would say to you in response?

Resources for reflection

Music

Listen to some music expressing confidence in God's care and protection; perhaps Bach's 'Sheep may safely graze'.

Silence

Poem

From the prison of anxious thought that greed has builded,
from the fetters that envy has wrought, and pride has gilded,
from the noise of the crowded ways and the fierce confusion,
from the folly that wastes its days in a world of illusion,
(ah, but the life is lost that frets and languishes there!)
I would escape and be free in the joy of the open air.

By the faith that the flowers show when they bloom unbidden,
by the calm of the river's flow to a goal that is hidden,
by the trust of the tree that clings to its deep foundation,
by the courage of wild birds' wings on the long migration,
(wonderful secret of peace that abides in Nature's breast!)
Teach me how to confide, and live my life, and rest.

Henry van Dyke (1852–1933)

Silence

Reflective prayer: The shopping trolley

She couldn't have managed without it,
    the weight of shopping simply too much
    for a woman of her years,
    but the trolley she pulled solved the problem,
    bearing a load she could never have carried alone –
    an impossible burden suddenly made light.

Thank you, Lord, that when I too wrestle with heavy loads,
    weighed down by problems that sap my strength
    and troubles that crush my spirit,
    you unfailingly come to my aid,
    helping to shoulder what I can no longer manage to bear.
Thank you for being there when I need you most,
    ready to carry not only the burden,
    but me as well.
Amen.

Silence

Like a dove come to me, fill me with peace;
Lord, I leave all in your care.
Time now for worry and striving to cease;
always, my God, you are there.
When strength is fading, you heal and renew,
where all seems hopeless, your hand sees me through,
though all else may fail me, your love will stay true:
always, my God, you are there.

Bind up my wounds and in love make me whole;
Lord, I leave all in your care.
Quieten my heart and bring rest to my soul;
always, my God, you are there.

When I am broken, you help me rebuild,
with you beside me the turmoil is stilled,
the darkest of moments with light will be filled:
always, my God, you are there.

Silence

Reflective prayer: The carnival

A carnival atmosphere, they called it . . .
    and it was –
    people dancing and singing in the streets,
    laughing, applauding, chatting and cheering,
    everywhere a sea of exuberant celebration.
For one day, at least, the drabness of life was swept away,
    replaced by a vibrant tapestry of sound and colour.

Lord, I have so much to celebrate,
    yet instead of rejoicing in all you have given,
    the countless blessings you so freely shower upon me,
    I brood over disappointments,
    fret about the future,
    complain about my lot
    and dwell on my troubles,
    until I can no longer see beyond them,
    my spirit closed to the generosity of your provision.
Forgive me,
    and teach me each day to exult in your awesome gift of life,
    now and for all eternity.
Amen.

Silence

Poem

When I'm feeling crushed by care,
heavy burdens hard to bear;
when my heart, oppressed by grief,
looks in vain to find relief;
when I find it hard to trust,
hopes and dreams reduced to dust;
teach me, Lord, that you are near,
never mind how things appear,
reaching out to see me through,
ever-faithful, ever-true.

Silence

Hymn text

What a friend we have in Jesus,
all our sins and griefs to bear!
What a privilege to carry
everything to God in prayer!
O what peace we often forfeit,
O what needless pain we bear,
all because we do not carry
everything to God in prayer.

Have we trials and temptations?
Is there trouble anywhere?
We should never be discouraged;
take it to the Lord in prayer.
Can we find a friend so faithful
who will all our sorrows share?
Jesus knows our every weakness;
take it to the Lord in prayer.

Are we weak and heavy laden,
cumbered with a load of care?
Precious Saviour, still our refuge;
take it to the Lord in prayer.
Do thy friends despise, forsake thee?
Take it to the Lord in prayer!
In his arms he'll take and shield thee;
thou wilt find a solace there.

Joseph Scriven (1819–86)

Silence

Proverbs and sayings

- Cast yourself into the arms of God and be very sure that if he wants anything of you, he will fit you for the work and give you strength. (St Philip Neri)

- Have courage for the great sorrows of life, and patience for the small ones. And when you have laboriously accomplished your daily task, go to sleep in peace. God is awake. (Victor Hugo)

- He who would have no trouble in this world must not be born in it. (Italian proverb)

- Adversity is the diamond dust heaven polishes its jewels with. (Anon)

- All things are less dreadful than they seem. (Arabian proverb)

- Courage and perseverance have a magical talisman, before which difficulties disappear and obstacles vanish into air. (John Quincy Adams)

- A needle is sharp only at one end. (Chinese proverb)

- What's the use of worrying? It was never worthwhile, so pack up your troubles in your old kit bag, and smile, smile, smile. (George Asaf (Powell))

Silence

Closing prayer

Deep peace of the running wave to you.
Deep peace of the flowing air to you.
Deep peace of the quiet earth to you.
Deep peace of the shining stars to you.
Deep peace of the infinite peace to you.

A Celtic blessing

Session 2

No time?

No time to stand beneath the boughs,
and stare as long as sheep and cows . . .

Aim

To reflect on our attitude towards time and to consider whether we can approach it differently.

Introductory verse

I trust in you, O Lord; I say, 'You are my God.' My times are in your hand. (Psalm 31:14, 15a)

Prayer

Lord,
    thank you for this time together –
    time set aside to pause, reflect, seek and learn.
You have time for us.
Teach us to make time for you.

Thank you for everything that fills our time –
   for work, hobbies, relationships and entertainment,
   each adding interest, pleasure and fulfilment to life –
   but save us from becoming slaves to these,
   rushing from one to the other with scarcely a moment's thought.
You have time for us.
Teach us to make time for you.

Thank you for times to come and times that have gone –
   those we look forward to with anticipation
   and others we remember with nostalgia –
   but save either the past or the future
   from ever overshadowing the present,
   preventing us from living each moment to the full.
You have time for us.
Teach us to make time for you.

Thank you for time with others –
   ordinary and special moments among family, friends,
   workmates or strangers –
   but in making time for them
   save us from leaving you shut outside.
You have time for us.
Teach us to make time for you.

Thank you that there's a time for everything –
   not perhaps conforming to *our* wishes,
   but subject to *yours*,
   and embraced in the context of eternity.
Save us, then, from chasing or resenting time,
   but let us see it rather as your gift.
You have time for us.
Teach us to make time for you.
Amen.

Introduction

'I'm sorry, but I haven't time' – those words have been spoken again and again. Asked to lend a hand, attend a meeting, support a project, we'll all have trotted them out as an excuse, with varying degrees of honesty. It may be, of course, that we *are* genuinely busy, our life a never-ending sequence of chasing schedules, meeting deadlines, rushing from one frenetic activity to the next. Equally, we may simply be busy doing our own thing – watching TV or socialising. In other words, we have plenty of time to give, if we really want to give it.

Time, in fact, is more complex than we sometimes realise. Scientists have proven that our perception of how fast it goes varies according to what we're doing, some moments seeming to flash by while others drag by interminably. And, paradoxically, the more we try to save time, the faster it can appear to go, until we truly come to believe we haven't a moment to spare. I'd like to focus here on two reasons for that in particular.

First, it's all too easy to allow rushing around to become a habit. Believe me, *I know*, for I've let that happen to me many times. We don't mean to do it, nor realise it's happening, but when we've a lot on our plate the temptation is to keep on doing that little bit extra, working first one evening, then another, then perhaps a weekend, and so on. Before we know it, we've eaten into time for leisure, time when we used to relax and unwind. As a result it becomes ever harder to switch off, and we end up feeling physically and emotionally drained. Life, if we're not careful, passes us by, for we find it increasingly difficult to look outside the closed world of what needs doing next.

Second, as the years pass we can become increasingly conscious of the clock ticking by in terms of our span of life. It dawns on us that we're not as young as we used to be, and whereas the future once seemed to stretch out indefinitely, suddenly it appears all too short, the time left to fulfil our dreams far less than we thought. We still have much we want to see and do, but not enough time in

23

which to do it, so, once again, we try to pack ever more into the unforgiving moment, convinced that we cannot afford to waste a single one. Instead of being a friend, time becomes our enemy, yet, try as we might, there's no way of countering its steady march or of turning back the clock.

How, then, are we to counter these destructive ways of approaching time? First, I think, we need to take life at a gentler pace instead of rushing around chasing our tails. Yes, there are things to do, problems to resolve and responsibilities to fulfil, but we can't tackle everything at once, no matter how hard we try. That job you're preoccupied with: is it so important it can't wait? That television programme on tonight: does it really matter if you miss it? That schedule you've set yourself: does it need to be quite so tight?

On the same lines, and as with our cares, we need to take life one day at a time and enjoy the given moment. So often we fret about what *may* happen but never does, failing to enjoy the here and now through brooding about what's to come. Yet can we ever change the future by worrying about it? Not according to Jesus. 'Which of you by worrying', he asked (Matthew 6:27), 'can add one cubit to your stature?' Far from helping us it will hinder, fears about the future destroying happiness in the present. Tomorrow will come soon enough, and when it does there will be time enough to deal with whatever it brings, but, until then, enjoy each moment while you have it and live it to the full.

What, though, about advancing years: how do we deal with that uncomfortable reality? For the Christian, faith brings a new perspective, this earthly life seen not as the totality of our experience but merely as a foretaste of things to come, one small step of our journey into God's eternity. The joys we know now are as nothing compared to those yet to come, any fulfilment this world might bring being dwarfed in relation to that which God holds in store. Death, in other words, is not the end of the story but the start of a new chapter and, in consequence, the passage of time should be seen in terms of promise rather than threat – as bringing us closer to our true and ultimate destiny in God's new creation.

Yet faith does not rest simply on future hope. It touches also the present moment, for, whatever our stage of life, God is able to transform the here and now. Of course, we will sometimes remember the past with a tinge of regret, or look to the future with a degree of anxiety, but his peace, love, strength and joy can shape every moment, if only we are open to his presence. The key is sorting out our priorities, putting God first and self second. Make time for him, and we may find we have more time than we realised.

Readings

Reflect quietly on the following passages of Scripture, considering what they have to say about your approach to and stewardship of time.

- Lord, you have been our home across the centuries. Before the mountains were formed and before you fashioned this world we live in, from eternity to eternity you are God. You return us to dust, saying, 'Back to what you once were, you mortals!' A thousand years are like a passing day in your sight, as short-lived as the night-watch. Our fleeting span is seventy years, perhaps eighty if we are strong; throughout they are filled with struggle and sorrow, here today and gone tomorrow. Teach us to make the most of our days and so to discover the secret of inner wisdom. (Psalm 90:1-4, 10, 12)

- There is a season for everything, and a time for every activity under heaven: a time to be born and a time to die; a time to plant and a time to uproot; a time to kill and a time to heal; a time to pull down and a time to build up; a time to cry and a time to laugh; a time to grieve and a time to dance; a time to scatter stones and a time to gather them; a time to embrace and a time not to embrace; a time to seek and a time to lose; a time to keep

25

and a time to throw away; a time to tear and a time to mend; a time for silence and a time for speech; a time to love and a time to hate; a time for war and a time for peace. (Ecclesiastes 3:1-8)

- This is the day that the Lord has made; let us celebrate and rejoice in it. (Psalm 118:24)

Discuss

- How much time do you give to your family? How much time to others? How much to work? How much to yourself? How much to God?

- How often do you feel rushed? Why? Is that feeling justified? Is there anything you can do about it? Do you often race about when you don't really need to?

- When did you last pause and reflect, doing nothing else? What stops you doing that? What helps you do so?

Resources for reflection

You may find it helpful in this session to focus for a time on a ticking clock, reflecting in doing so on the passage of time and what this says to you of God.

Reflective prayer

'Do you have the time?' he asked,
   and I was more than happy to answer,
   but though I told him the minute and hour,
   I *didn't* have the time,
   not *really*,
   not in the sense that matters most.
I'd no time for the beggar busking on the street corner,
   for the pensioner struggling with her shopping
   or for the student distributing the flyers;
   no time to write that letter,
   make that phone call
   or visit that lonely neighbour;
   no time to get involved with the local cause,
   respond to the national campaign,
   support the global charity;
   no time to relax,
   unwind
   or take stock;
   no time, in fact, for anything but chasing my tail.

Lord, despite my rushing round in circles,
   I could achieve far more,
   if only I were to get my priorities right
   and focus on the things that matter.
So little of what I do is as pressing as I think
   and so much gets me nowhere.
Teach me to *make* time –
   for me,
   for others
   and for you.
Amen.

Silence

27

Meditation

Time is . . .
too slow for those who wait,
too swift for those who fear,
too long for those who grieve,
too short for those who rejoice,
but for those who love,
Time is Eternity.

Henry van Dyke (1852–1933)

Silence

Reflective prayer

When as a child I laughed and wept,
    time crept.
When as a youth I waxed more bold,
    time *strolled*.
When I became a full-grown man,
    time RAN.
When older still I daily grew,
    time FLEW.
Soon I shall find, in passing on,
    time GONE.
O Christ! wilt thou have saved me then?
Amen.

Lines found above an old clock in Chester Cathedral

Silence

Reflective prayer: The bluebell woods

What a sight!
What a scent!
What an unforgettable picture they made!
Soon over, it's true,
    but for the month they were in bloom
    each delicate head nodding in the breeze,
    they turned the woodland into an ocean of colour and fragrance,
    a glimpse of Eden,
    a foretaste of paradise I will never forget.

Lord, our human span,
    like the bluebell's,
    is all too brief,
    in the context of the universe just a passing moment,
    a fleeting shadow.
Help me to make the most of the time you give me,
    celebrating each moment and,
    in my own small way,
    reflecting something of your love and glory,
    until that day when I do not merely glimpse paradise
    but behold it in all its glory.
Amen.

Silence

Meditation

God, I'm busy,
    rushed off my feet,
    running around like a headless chicken
    with scarcely a moment to breathe.
I hardly know what I'm doing one day to the next,
    always something else waiting,

29

someone else demanding my time –
   another job,
   another need,
   another cry for help.
Lord, I'm exhausted,
   just about fit to drop,
   for I've given everything.
Yet I can't afford to stop,
   not yet anyway,
   for if I do, who will pick up the pieces –
   who will ensure the job gets done?
I've done my best –
   no one can argue with that –
   but there's so much still to do
   and so little time to do it.
Lord, give me strength,
   give me a break,
   give me something!

My child,
   you are busy,
   your energy astonishing –
   I honestly don't know how you do it!
But be careful, please,
   for even *you* need to stop some time.
You can't take on everything, and you mustn't try,
   however strong the urge may be.
I know it's hard to leave a job undone,
   a task unfinished,
   but occasionally you need to, or you'll pay the price –
   believe me, I've seen it all too often.
So step back a little,
   and think about what you're doing and why you're doing it.
Is it really so urgent?
Won't it wait till tomorrow?

Does it have to be you?
You see, sometimes we can be so busy
   we lose sight of what really matters.
There's a time for busyness, don't get me wrong,
   for *doing* instead of simply talking,
   but there's a time also for being still
   and reflecting on what really counts.
So stop a minute and pause for breath,
   for perhaps then,
   and only then,
   you may find the rest you crave.

Silence

Reflective prayer: The stopwatch

They were racing against the clock,
   every millisecond counting,
   so the athletes strained forward,
   limbs pumping,
   lungs bursting,
   determined to set a new fastest time.

The older I get, Lord, the more life feels like that,
   as though the stopwatch is running and time is running out,
   so I rush around from one thing to the next,
   determined to cram ever more into the unforgiving minute.
Yet so easily, in my haste, I forget to enjoy what I have,
   to let go of striving and simply to live.
Remind me that though this mortal span may be slipping away,
   it is just a taste of things to come;
   that though the days are passing, I have no cause to fret,
   for with you I have all the time in the world . . .
   and far, far beyond!
Amen.

Silence

Poem

I saw Eternity the other night
like a great Ring of pure and endless light,
all calm as it was bright;
and round beneath it, Time in hours, days, years,
driven by the spheres
like a vast shadow moved, in which the world
and all her train were hurled.

Henry Vaughan (1622–95)

Silence

Meditation

Take time to think . . . it is the source of power.
Take time to play . . . it is the secret of perpetual youth.
Take time to read . . . it is the fountain of wisdom.
Take time to pray . . . it is the greatest power on earth.
Take time to love and be loved . . . it is a God-given privilege.
Take time to be friendly . . . it is the road to happiness.
Take time to laugh . . . it is the music of the soul.
Take time to give . . . it is too short a day to be selfish.
Take time to work . . . it is the price of success.
Take time to do charity . . . it is the key to heaven.

Anon

Silence

Proverbs and sayings

- He who neglects the present moment throws away all he has. (Schiller)

- Time and tide, as they say, wait for no one. (Traditional)

- Time deals gently with those who take it gently. (Anatole France)

- More haste, less speed. (Traditional)

- One always has time enough if one will apply it. (Goethe)

- Time is full of eternity. As we use it so shall we be. (Henry Manning)

- One day at a time – this is enough. Do not look back and grieve over the past, for it is gone; and do not be troubled about the future, for it has not yet come. Live in the present, and make it so beautiful it will be worth remembering. (Anon)

- Your destination will still be there when you arrive. (Anon)

- We are so obsessed with doing that we have no time and no imagination left for being. (Thomas Merton)

- If your business keeps you so busy that you have no time for anything else, there must be something wrong, either with you or with your business. (William J. H. Boetcker)

- People who have a lot of money and no time we call 'rich'. People who have time but no money we call 'poor'. Yet the most precious gifts – love, friendship, time with loved ones – grow only in the sweet soil of 'unproductive' time. (Anon)

Silence

Closing prayer

Lord, help me to realise today that you will be speaking to me
    through the events of the day,
    through people,
    through things,
    and through all creation.
Give me ears, eyes and heart to perceive you,
    however veiled your presence may be.
Give me insight to see through the exterior of things
    to the interior truth.
Give me your Spirit of discernment.
O Lord, you know how busy I must be this day.
If I forget you, do not forget me.
Amen.

Jacob Astley (1579–1652), prayed during the English Civil War, just before the Battle of Edgehill in 1642

Session 3
Streams full of stars

No time to see, in broad daylight,
streams full of stars, like skies at night . . .

Aim

To reflect on how aspects of everyday life can point beyond themselves and above all to God.

Introductory verse

Do you still not understand or realise what is happening? Have your hearts become so hardened that despite having eyes you cannot see and having ears you cannot hear? (Mark 8:17b, 18)

Prayer

Lord,
   we yearn to know you better,
   to understand your way and honour your will.
We hunger to walk with you,
   not just in moments of worship
   but every minute of the day.
Help us to recognise your presence,
   everywhere and in everything.

Speak to us here,
   through reading and prayer,
   prose and poetry,
   and through the fellowship we share together.
Help us to recognise your presence,
   everywhere and in everything.

Speak through our homes,
   our leisure time
   and our places of work,
   teaching, challenging, inspiring and rebuking.
Help us to recognise your presence,
   everywhere and in everything.

Speak through the events of life,
   its joys and sorrows,
   triumphs and disappointments,
   renewing your call and revealing your love.
Help us to recognise your presence,
   everywhere and in everything.

Speak through places and people,
   words and deeds –
   through all we encounter and experience.
Help us to recognise your presence,
   everywhere and in everything.
Amen.

Introduction

'Streams full of stars' – what a lovely image. At once it transports us to some bubbling brook or gurgling mountain stream, every ripple catching the sun's rays so that the water seems to twinkle like the night sky. Is that all the poet intended by his metaphor?

Probably, but his words bring home to me how, just as the brilliance of day can call to mind the grandeur of night, so also much else around us can point beyond itself, speaking of altogether different realities. Even the most everyday things of life can suddenly take on a wholly unsuspected dimension: the song of a bird, cry of a baby, sight of a rainbow, pattern of a snowflake, sound of the sea, or simple beauty of a flower. Special in themselves, they speak to some of the wonder of our universe, to others of a spiritual dimension, and to others again, of God.

An old saying makes the point well: 'Two men looked out through prison bars; one saw mud, the other saw stars.' I like that. Instead of seeing ugliness we can see beauty: reason to hope instead of despair. That's not to say everything is subjective; rather that, on occasions, our minds must first be opened if we're to appreciate the full wonder of what's there in front of us. Isn't that what Jesus was saying in his celebrated words on the mountainside: 'See how the lilies of the field grow. They do not labour or spin, yet I tell you that not even Solomon in all his grandeur was clothed like one of these. If that is how God clothes the grass of the field, which is here today yet tomorrow is thrown on to the fire, will he not much more clothe you, O you of little faith?' (Matthew 6:28-30). Look properly at the ordinary things of life, Jesus tells us – things as commonplace as a flower in the meadow – and you will see God's hand behind them – a truth he applied in so much of his teaching, using parables and metaphors to illustrate profound truths. To the eye of faith, the apparently mundane can take on a completely new dimension, speaking not just of the wonder of this world but also of God.

In his poem, Davies clearly had the world of nature in mind, and with good reason for, as we'll explore in our next session, it can speak powerfully indeed, but so also can anything and everything to those who are ready to stop and stare. To borrow the idea of John Donne, no one is an island sufficient to themselves; our lives are interconnected, our world a complex network of relationships. The sight of a supermarket, for example, might speak of farming and food production, trade and economic issues, environmental concerns, the international community, Sunday trading, or out-of-town shopping. A doctor's surgery may speak of childless couples, expectant mothers, the terminally ill, medical research or God's healing touch. A school may speak of young people, the privilege of learning, the importance of discipline, or unfathomed mysteries. And so we could go on. But we will only make the connections if we are ready to look, and to do that we must learn to stop and stare – to pause, in other words, during the press of a busy day, and see *beyond* ourselves and *beneath* the surface. That's why it's so important to make time and space in our lives: for ourselves, for others and for God. Learn to make room for all and we will see life in a new light and God in all of life.

Readings

Reflect quietly on the following passages of Scripture, considering what they have to say to you about glimpsing God in daily life.

- Look at the birds of the air; they do not sow or reap or store away in barns, and yet your heavenly Father feeds them. Are you not much more valuable than they? See how the lilies of the field grow. They do not labour or spin, yet I tell you that not even Solomon in all his grandeur was clothed like one of these. If that is how God clothes the grass of the field, which is here today yet tomorrow is thrown on to the fire, will he not much more clothe you, O you of little faith? (Matthew 6:26, 28-30)

- Asked by the Pharisees about the coming of the kingdom of God, he replied: 'The signs of God's kingdom cannot be observed, nor will anyone say, "Look here!" or "Look there!" – for the kingdom of God is within you.' (Luke 17:20, 21)

Discuss

- What ordinary things in life have spoken to you most power-fully of God? What things have spoken *unexpectedly* of him, and in what ways?

- How far do you see God as involved in the daily affairs of life, and, again, in what ways? Do you relegate him to the world of 'religion' or see him as equally involved in the world of work, commerce, sport, leisure and so forth? How far, in other words, does your faith extend from Sunday to the rest of the week?

- The flipside of the theme we've been exploring in this session is that everyday things can speak *against* God and apparently undermine our faith. Has that been true for you? In what ways? How did you come to terms with such moments?

Resources for reflection

You may find it helpful in this session to spend a short time walking reflectively around the neighbourhood and quietly considering what things might speak there of God.

Music

Listen to a piece of music that speaks of seeing the world or life in a new light; perhaps 'O for the wings of a dove' by Felix Mendelssohn.

Silence

Poem

To see a world in a grain of sand
and a heaven in a wild flower,
hold infinity in the palm of your hand
and eternity in an hour.

William Blake (1757–1827)

Silence

Extract

I, the fiery life of divine wisdom,
I ignite the beauty of the plains,
I sparkle the waters,
I burn in the sun, and the moon, and the stars.
With wisdom I order all rightly.

Hildegard of Bingen (1098–1179)

Silence

Reflective prayer: The sermon

He knew his stuff, I'll give him that,
    and he could probably have recited the Bible word for word
    and back to front,
    yet the message left me cold,
    for it stayed up in the clouds
    and never touched down,
    too much concerned with heaven,
    too little with earth.

Lord, set my heart on things above,
  but keep my faith firmly on the ground,
  relevant to daily life,
  shaping the things I think and say and do.
Touch the ordinary with the wonder of your presence,
  so that each moment might speak of you
  and be lived in the light of your love.
Amen.

Silence

Extract

I feel that a man may be happy in this world and I know that this world is a world of imagination and vision. I see everything I paint in this world, but everybody does not see alike. To the eye of a miser, a guinea is far more beautiful that the sun, and a bag worn with the use of money has more beautiful proportions than a vine filled with grapes. The tree which moves some to tears of joy is, in the eyes of others, only a green thing which stands in the way. As a man is, so he sees.
William Blake (1757–1827)

Silence

Reflective prayer: The caged bird
It was a sad sight:
  a bird that should have soared and wheeled above
  tied instead to earth,
  not only caged but its wings clipped,

41

never again to be unfurled in earnest
and ride upon the breeze.

There are times, Lord, when *my* wings *need* clipping,
    in order to take me down a bit,
    but save me from becoming so tied to this world
    that I am unable to rise above the petty and mundane.
Liberate my spirit
    that I may climb to you on eagle's wings,
    catching a vision of what life can be,
    what I can do
    and what you are doing –
    a glimpse of the special in the ordinary,
    the sacred in the secular,
    the divine in the daily round of life.
Amen.

Silence

Extract

Love all God's creation, both the whole and every grain of sand. Love every leaf, every ray of light. Love the animals, love the plants, love each separate thing. If you love each thing, you will perceive the mystery of God in all; and when once you perceive this, you will from that time on grow every day to a fuller understanding of it until you come at last to love the whole world with a love that will then be all-embracing and universal.

Fyodor Dostoevsky (1821–81)

Silence

Proverbs and sayings

- Much of what we see depends on what we are looking for. (Anon)

- Lay hold of God in all things and this will be a sign of your birth, a sign that God has given birth in you as the only begotten Son, and nothing less. (Meister Eckhart)

- If the doors of perception were cleansed, everything would appear as it is – infinite. (William Blake)

- Everything has its beauty, but not everyone sees it. (Confucius)

- In my understanding I saw God in a point. In seeing this I saw that God is in all things. God works in creatures because God is in the mid-point of everything. (Julian of Norwich)

- God often visits us, but most of the time we are not at home. (French proverb)

- When you take a flower in your hand and really look at it, it's your world for the moment. I want to give that world to someone else. Most people in the city rush around so, they have no time to look at a flower. I want them to see it whether they want to or not. (Georgia O'Keeffe)

- The day of my spiritual awakening was the day I saw and knew I saw all things in God and God in all things. (Mechtild of Magdeburg)

- Life becomes precious and more special to us when we look for the little everyday miracles and get excited about the privileges of simply being human. (Tim Hansel)

- The universe is but one vast symbol of God. (Thomas Carlyle)

- There are only two ways to live your life. One is as though nothing is a miracle. The other is as though everything is a miracle. (Albert Einstein)

- It is God whom human beings know in every creature. (Hildegard of Bingen)

- The veil that clouds your eyes shall be lifted by the hands that wove it. (Kahlil Gibran)

- Those things that nature denied to human sight, she revealed to the eyes of the soul. (Ovid)

- Every beauty which is seen here below by persons of perception resembles more than anything else that celestial source from which we all are come. (Michelangelo)

- There is another reality enfolding ours – as close as our breath! (Don Pendleton)

Silence

Closing prayer

Lord, help me to think of my small, formless, imperfect soul
    as constantly subject to your loving, creative action,
    here and now, in all the bustle of my daily life,
    its ups and downs,
    its anxieties and tensions
    and its dreary, unspiritual stretches –
    and gradually giving it, through these things,
    its ordained form and significance.
So that in all the events of my life,
    even the most trivial,
    I experience your pressure,
    Creative Artist.
Amen.
Evelyn Underhill (1875–1941)

Session 4

Nature's dance

No time to turn at Beauty's glance,
and watch her feet, how they can dance . . .

Aim

To reflect on the beauty of the natural world.

Introductory verses

He shrouds the sky in cloud and prepares rain for the earth; he bedecks the hills with grass and foliage. He causes the snow to fall, white as wool, and sprinkles frost thick as ashes; he scatters hail like crumbs of bread; he sends cold, and pools of water freeze over; he speaks his word, and the ice melts; he makes the wind blow and the waters flow again. (Psalm 147:8, 16-18)

Prayer

Lord,
    you have given us an enchanting world,
    full of beauty and variety,
    able to enthral, amaze and inspire beyond measure.
Teach us to appreciate the awesome wonder of your creation,
    and through it to appreciate you.

Forgive us for overlooking its loveliness,
   growing over-familiar,
   taking for granted what once stirred our hearts
   and captured our imagination.
Teach us to appreciate the awesome wonder of your creation,
   and through it to appreciate you.

Forgive us for being so absorbed
   by our various concerns and problems
   that we see little else;
   for being too busy to stop and stare,
   rushing frenetically instead from one thing to another
   and consequently losing sight of life's simple treasures.
Teach us to appreciate the awesome wonder of your creation,
   and through it to appreciate you.

Open our hearts afresh to the loveliness of creation,
   the awesomeness of the universe,
   the abundance of this Earth
   and the loveliness that everywhere surrounds us,
   and so rekindle in us a childlike sense of wonder and gratitude.
Teach us to appreciate the awesome wonder of your creation,
   and through it to appreciate you.
Amen.

Introduction

We opened the bird-hide windows and looked out eagerly, our expectation heightened by the sighting reported that week, but there was nothing – not even a feather in view. Ten minutes later and we were still waiting and about to give up, when a movement in the bushes caught our eye. What was it? A woodpecker, nuthatch, warbler? Perhaps even a crossbill or flycatcher? No, it was none of these – just an ordinary sparrow.

I say ordinary, but that's wrong, for if you take time to look at a sparrow properly – particularly a tree or house sparrow – you'll discover it's actually a remarkably beautiful bird, its plumage a wonderful mixture of brown, grey and blue in a bewildering variety of shades. Each is a work of art, a living miracle that should cause us to catch our breath in wonder, but, as with many things, that doesn't always happen. Partly that's down to familiarity, the more we see something – no matter how beautiful – the more blasé we become about it. I've a framed picture in my living room, for example, which, when we first bought it, I would gaze at repeatedly, delighting in the pastoral scene it portrays. Now, though, I pass it by without a second thought, barely even registering that it's there. It must be months, even years, since I last stopped and really looked at that picture, observing the details that first caught my eye.

This brings us to a second point: that we can fail to see sometimes because we fail to look. As I write, for example, I've come down into the garden where I'm surrounded by flowerbeds full of colour as the sun pours down from a cloudless sky. I've 'seen' the plants out of the corner of my eye for the last ten minutes or so, but only now have I paused to look: to drink in the vibrant shades of red, yellow, green and blue; to marvel at the beauty of the blooms, so perfectly formed and delicately patterned; to savour the sweet scent of pinks, lavender, jasmine and honeysuckle; to witness the way the stems rock gently to and fro in the breeze. Suddenly I'm aware of stunning beauty all around me – beauty that a moment ago I'd overlooked. That's what happens if we don't make time to stop and stare: we let beauty pass unnoticed, settling for a tunnel vision that sees only in part.

Of course, not everything in the natural world is beautiful – not by a long way. I can see now a slug reducing a plant to a few tattered leaves, an infestation of black fly smothering another with sticky residue, a spider consuming a hapless bluebottle, a blackbird with its mouth stuffed full of worms – all this a reminder that nature is, as they say, red in tooth and claw, with its fair share of ugliness. Yet it is a marvel nonetheless, able to captivate, enthral, intrigue and inspire so that we catch our breath in wonder and sing for joy. It puts us in touch with ourselves while simultaneously taking us outside our limited horizons, placing the whole of life in a different context. It speaks of the sheer miracle of life, so special yet so easily forgotten. Whatever your cares, whatever the limitations on your time, pause once in a while to celebrate what God has given in the world around you, and you will not be disappointed.

Readings

Reflect quietly on the following passages of Scripture, considering what they have to say to you about glimpsing God in the natural world.

- Sovereign Lord, how magnificent is your name throughout this world. Your glory fills the universe and exceeds it. When I gaze at the heavens, your handiwork, the moon and stars that you brought into being, what are human beings that you bother with them, mortals that they matter to you? Yet, you have made them scarcely less than divine and crowned them with glory and honour. You have given them authority over your creation and put all things under their feet. (Psalm 8:1, 3-6)

- The heavens extol the glory of God; and the firmament testifies to his handiwork. Day after day bears eloquent witness, and night after night communicates knowledge, without any need of speech, language or any other voice. Their music pervades all the earth; their words reach out to the furthest parts of the world. (Psalm 19:1-4)

- Are not five sparrows sold for a couple of pence? Yet God does not overlook a single one of them. Believe me, the very hairs of your head are numbered. Never fear, then, for you mean even more to him than many sparrows. (Luke 12:6, 7)

- The earth is the Lord's and everything in it, the world and all those who live in it. In his hand are the innermost parts of the earth, and the mountain peaks belong to him. The sea is his, for he made it, and his hands shaped the dry land. (Psalm 24:1; 95:4, 5)

Discuss

- What aspects of creation most cause you to catch your breath in wonder? A spectacular sunset perhaps, a thunderstorm, a stormy sea, a rainbow, the view from a mountaintop, the sight of a newborn baby, the sky at night, spring flowers? Can you recall particular moments when you were held spellbound by a sight, sound or scent in the natural world?

- How often do you pause and gaze at natural phenomena? Do you do so as often as you'd like to? If not, what stops you? Is the problem one of lack of time or over-familiarity?

- In what ways does the natural world speak to you of God? In what ways does it challenge your faith?

Resources for reflection

You may again find it helpful in this session to spend a short time in a local park or garden, reflecting on the beauty of nature and what it says of God.

Music

Listen to a piece of music celebrating the wonder of creation; perhaps Louis Armstrong singing 'What a wonderful world', or the chorus 'The heavens are telling' from Haydn's *Creation*, or the popular song 'A nightingale sang in Berkeley Square'.

Silence

Poem

I wandered lonely as a cloud
that floats on high o'er vales and hills,
when all at once I saw a crowd,
a host, of golden daffodils;
beside the lake, beneath the trees,
fluttering and dancing in the breeze.

Continuous as the stars that shine
and twinkle on the milky way,
they stretched in never-ending line
along the margin of a bay:
ten thousand saw I at a glance,
tossing their heads in sprightly dance.

The waves beside them danced; but they
out-did the sparkling waves in glee:
a poet could not but be gay,
in such a jocund company:
I gazed – and gazed – but little thought
what wealth the show to me had brought:

For oft, when on my couch I lie
in vacant or in pensive mood,
they flash upon that inward eye
which is the bliss of solitude;
and then my heart with pleasure fills,
and dances with the daffodils.

William Wordsworth (1770–1850)

Silence

Prayer

When I look at your heavens,
   according to my own lights,
   with these weak eyes of mine,
   I am certain without reservation that they are your heavens.
The stars circle in the heavens,
   reappear year after year,
   each with a function and service to fulfil.
And though I do not understand them,
   I know that you, O God, are in them.
Amen.

Hilary of Poitiers (315–67)

Silence

Poem

O world, I cannot hold thee close enough!
Thy winds, thy wide grey skies!
Thy mists, that roll and rise!
Thy woods, this autumn day, that ache and sag
and all but cry with colour! That gaunt crag
to crush! To lift the lean of that black bluff!
World, world, I cannot get thee close enough!

Long have I known a glory in it all
but never knew I this.
Here such a passion is
as stretcheth me apart. Lord, I do fear
thou'st made the world too beautiful this year.
My soul is all but out of me – let fall
no burning leaf; prithee, let no bird call.

'God's World', Edna St Vincent Millay (1892–1950)

51

Silence

Prayer

Thank you, O God,
   for the pleasures you have given me through my senses.
Thank you for the glory of thunder,
   the mystery of music,
   the singing of birds
   and the laughter of children.
Thank you for the delights of colour,
   the awe of sunset,
   the wild roses in the hedgerows,
   the smile of friendship.
Thank you for the sweetness of flowers
   and the scent of hay.
Truly, O Lord, the earth is full of your riches!
Amen.

Bishop Edward King (1829–1910)

Silence

Poem

There is a pleasure in the pathless woods,
there is a rapture on the lonely shore,
there is society, where none intrudes,
by the deep sea, and music in its roar:
I love not man the less, but Nature more,
from these our interviews, in which I steal
from all I may be, or have been before,
to mingle with the Universe, and feel
what I can ne'er express, yet cannot all conceal.

Lord Byron (1788–1824)

Silence

Reflective prayer: The rose

It was beautiful, Lord,
  more lovely than I'd ever begun to realise –
  a single rose,
  newly opened,
  still wet with the morning dew –
  and I stood there gazing,
  utterly enchanted by its simple perfection.
Another flower, that's how I'd seen it before,
  pleasant enough,
  attractive,
  yet hardly wonderful.
But now, as I stooped to view it closely,
  as I caught its perfume and noted each delicate petal,
  I glimpsed a miracle,
  a work of art,
  an astonishing labour of love.
And I saw *you* there, Lord,
  your hand,
  your presence –
  the gentleness of your touch,
  the order of your mind,
  the tenderness of your heart.
I saw your love expressed in that one fragile bloom,
  symbol of a world put together with inexpressible care –
  a world full of delight,
  able to stir our imagination and thrill our hearts,
  to move and inspire us beyond words,
  to touch our souls with a taste of heaven.

My child,
  you think it beautiful, that flower?

I'm glad, for it's meant to be,
    though all too few see it.
But if you think that's special,
    look around you at this world I've made –
    its diversity of life,
    its variety and interest,
    so endlessly complex,
    so infinitely fascinating.
Look at the sky –
    the glow of the sun,
    the twinkle of the stars,
    the vastness of the heavens.
And, most of all, look at yourself and your fellow human beings –
    your awesome array of talents,
    your incredible potential,
    the amazing miracle of human life.
Here too is beauty,
    most astonishing of all.
In the laughter of a child and the vigour of youth,
    in the embrace of lovers and the joy of parents,
    in the experience of maturity and the wisdom of age,
    I am present,
    for you are all the work of my hands,
    a testimony to my purpose,
    a reminder of my never-failing love.
So look again, my child, at that simple flower,
    at the loveliness of this world,
    only see there not just the splendour of *me*,
    but the wonder of *you*!

Silence

Poem

The beauty of dew in the morning
and the chorus of birds in the trees,
the thrill of a new day dawning,
the hum of life on the breeze;
so much within creation
enthuses and uplifts.
O Lord, you bring elation
through all your many gifts.

Through the peace of twilight falling,
the sun setting low in the sky,
the sound of a blackbird calling,
the sparkling stars on high;
through these, O Lord, you bless us,
your power in each displayed.
Receive my praise and worship
for all that you have made.

Silence

Poem

. . . For I have learned
to look on nature, not as in the hour
of thoughtless youth; but hearing oftentimes
the still sad music of humanity,
nor harsh nor grating, though of ample power
to chasten and subdue. And I have felt
a presence that disturbs me with the joy
of elevated thoughts; a sense sublime
of something far more deeply interfused,
whose dwelling is the light of setting suns,
and the round ocean and the living air,
and the blue sky, and in the mind of man:

55

a motion and a spirit, that impels
all thinking things, all objects of all thought,
and rolls through all things. Therefore am I still
a lover of the meadows and the woods,
and mountains; and of all that we behold
from this green earth; of all the mighty world
of eye, and ear both what they half create,
and what perceive; well pleased to recognise
in nature and the language of the sense
the anchor of my purest thoughts, the nurse,
the guide, the guardian of my heart, and soul
of all my moral being.

From 'Lines Composed above Tintern Abbey',
William Wordsworth (1770–1850)

Silence

Prayer

May none of God's wonderful works keep silence,
    night or morning.
Bright stars,
    high mountains,
    the depths of the seas,
    sources of rushing rivers:
    may all these break into song
    as we sing to the Father, Son and Holy Spirit.
May all the angels in the heavens reply:
    Amen, Amen, Amen.
Power, praise, honour, eternal glory to God,
    the only giver of grace.
Amen, Amen, Amen.

Anon (3rd to 6th century AD)

Silence

Poem

I think that I shall never see
a poem lovely as a tree.
A tree whose hungry mouth is prest
against the earth's sweet flowing breast;
a tree that looks at God all day,
and lifts her leafy arms to pray;
a tree that may in Summer wear
a nest of robins in her hair;
upon whose bosom snow has lain;
who ultimately lives with rain.
Poems are made by fools like me,
but only God can make a tree.

Joyce Kilmer, a US soldier killed in action shortly before the end of the First World War

Silence

Extract

'What is this God?' I asked the earth, and it answered, 'I am not he,' and all things that are in the earth made the same confession. I asked the sea and the deeps and the creeping things, and they answered, 'We are not your God; seek higher . . .'

I asked the heavens, the sun, the moon, the stars, and they answered, 'Neither are we the God whom you seek.' And I said to all the things that throng about the gateways of the senses, 'Tell me something of him.' And they cried out in a great voice, 'He made us.' My question was my gazing upon them, and their answer was their beauty . . . I asked the whole frame of the universe about my God and it answered me, 'I am not he but he made me.'

'Confessions', St Augustine of Hippo (354–430)

57

Silence

Poem

In a garden green and gay,
all my troubles fade away.
Sweet contentment here I find,
joy of heart and peace of mind.
Patience Strong (1907–90)

Silence

Proverbs and sayings

- Nature is the art of God. (Latin proverb)
- All through my life the new sights of Nature made me rejoice like a child. (Marie Curie)
- A monk asks: 'Is there anything more miraculous than the wonders of nature?' The Master answers: 'Yes, your awareness of the wonders of nature.' (Anon)
- Nature is the living, visible garment of God. (Goethe)
- Wonder is the basis of worship. (Thomas Carlyle)
- Posterity will some day laugh at the foolishness of modern materialistic philosophy. The more I study nature, the more I am amazed at the Creator. (Louis Pasteur)
- There can be no very black misery to him who lives in the midst of nature and has his senses still. (Henry David Thoreau)
- Every flower of the field, every fibre of a plant, every particle of an insect, carries with it the impress of its Maker, and can – if duly considered – read us lectures of ethics or divinity. (Thomas Pope Blount)

- You will find something far greater in the woods than you will in books. Stones and trees will teach you what you can never learn from masters. (St Bernard)

- Nature has some perfections, to show that she is the image of God; and some defects, to show that she is only his image. (Pascal)

- Come forth into the light of things – let nature be your teacher. (William Wordsworth)

- Nature is an unlimited broadcasting station, through which God speaks to us every hour, if we only will tune in. (George Washington Carver)

Silence

Closing prayer

O God, I thank you for this universe;
    for its vastness and its riches,
    and for the variety of life which teems within it
    and of which I am a part.
I praise you for the sky and the winds,
    for the clouds
    and for the constellation of the heavens.
I praise you for seas and rivers,
    for mountains and trees,
    and the grass beneath my feet.
I thank you for the senses
    which enable me to see the splendour of the morning,
    to hear the song of the birds,
    and to enjoy the scents of springtime.

Open my heart, I pray,
  to all this joy and beauty,
  and save me from being so burdened by care
  or blinded by greed
  that I fail to notice when even the thorn bushes
  are aflame with your glory.
Amen.

Walter Rauschenbusch (1861–1918)

Session 5

Stand and stare

A poor life this if, full of care,
we have no time to stand and stare.

Aim

To reflect on the need to stop and stare, and, through this session,
to do just that.

Introductory verse

Be still, and recognise that I am God. (Psalm 46:10)

Prayer

God of peace,
    thank you for quiet moments in our lives –
    opportunities to pause and ponder,
    relax and reflect.
In the bustle of daily life,
    teach us to stop and stare.
Thank you for breaks in the busy routine of life –
    times when the pressures ease,

the responsibilities lessen
and the workload is lightened.
In the bustle of daily life,
   teach us to stop and stare.

Thank you for special moments of tranquillity –
   the stillness of the sky at night,
   the sound of birds singing,
   the view from a mountaintop,
   the gentle murmur of a stream –
   so much in this world you have given
   bringing quietness to the spirit
   and rest to the mind.
In the bustle of daily life,
   teach us to stop and stare.

Thank you for opportunities to step aside
   from the fevered activity of life –
   times of worship,
   retreat,
   meditation
   and personal devotion.
In the bustle of daily life,
   teach us to stop and stare.

Thank you for the inner stillness you alone can give –
   a quietness of mind,
   contentment of spirit
   and peace that passes understanding.
In the bustle of daily life,
   teach us to stop and stare.

For everything that helps us
   to be still and know that you are God,
   thank you.
Amen.

Introduction

One of the ways I find time to write is by making the most of every spare moment, to the point of carrying a Dictaphone with me when I'm out walking so that I can record any ideas that come to mind. The other day, however, I forgot to pick it up, so I was able, for a change, to focus my thoughts on the things around me: the sound of the birds in the trees, the feel of the sun and gentleness of the breeze, the scent of wild flowers growing by the roadside and the sight of clouds drifting overhead. I realised suddenly how often I pass those by without taking them in, my mind so preoccupied with other concerns that I overlook the countless blessings that daily surround me if only I have eyes to see and ears to hear.

That, of course, has been the theme of this book – the need to stop and stare. We've considered this in various contexts: getting our problems into proper perspective, coping with pressures of time, glimpsing God's presence in everyday life and seeing him above all in the wonder of nature. In this, our final session, I want to pull those strands together, emphasising the importance of quiet contemplation both for our personal well-being and for nourishing our relationship with God.

We *need* quietness more than we might think, but in our modern world it's become something of a luxury, so rarely encountered that some people find it disconcerting, even intimidating. Our lives are filled with noise – the roar of traffic in our streets; the clatter of machinery at the factory; the buzz of computers, telephones and fax machines in the office; the blaring of radios, televisions and hi-fi systems at home – all this and so much more adds up to a daily bombardment of sound. Not only can that wear us down but, more insidiously, it can prevent us from ever pausing to take stock, to commune with our own soul and, above all, to be still before God.

It's noticeable that Jesus himself seems to have made regular time for quietness, drawing away from the crowds to spend time alone so that he could focus on his Father, away from the innumerable pressures and demands put upon him. Many of the great Christian mystics likewise recognised the importance of such times, spending hours, days, even weeks in silent and isolated contemplation. That may be neither practical nor appealing for most of us, but we need at least a little of such quietness if we are to grow truly close to God.

It's not that he's removed from the daily round of life – far from it – but sometimes his presence is obscured by hustle, bustle, noise and clamour. When the children are screaming and there's a pile of washing-up to see to, when there's another meeting to attend and another deadline to meet, when there's a problem we can't see a solution to or a fear that haunts us, stepping back can seem a luxury we can ill afford. Yet the truth is we cannot afford *not* to, for only then will we learn the secret of inner tranquillity, the peace of God that passes all understanding.

Readings

Reflect quietly on the following passages of Scripture, considering what they have to say to you about being still so as to make time and space for God.

- It is preferable to have just a little, and peace of mind, than to be constantly busy, hands always at work, attempting to catch the wind. (Ecclesiastes 4:6)

- Martha was preoccupied with her many tasks; so she came to him and asked, 'Lord, doesn't it matter to you that my sister has left me to do all the work by myself? Tell her to lend a hand.' But the Lord answered her, 'Martha, Martha, you are fretting and distracted by many things; only one thing is really important. Mary has chosen that more important thing, and it will not be taken away from her.' (Luke 10:40-42)

- He told his disciples to get into the boat and go on ahead of him to Bethsaida, on the other side, while he dismissed the crowd. After taking leave of them, he went up on the mountain to pray. (Mark 6:45, 46)

- In those days he went out to the mountain to pray; and all night he continued in prayer to God. (Luke 6:12)

- So says the Lord God, the Holy One of Israel: Return to me, be calm, and you will be safe; your strength lies in quiet trust. (Isaiah 30:15)

Discuss

- How often do you spend time in silent reflection before God? Do you find silence helpful or do you feel the need to fill it? What are the advantages of silence? What are the disadvantages?

- What do you understand by 'quiet times'? What gets in the way of them? Do you make as much time for them as you should? If not, what stops you doing so?

- What do you find helpful as aids to reflection? What suggestions would you give to others in cultivating a more contemplative lifestyle and relationship with God?

Resources for reflection

You may find it helpful in this session to observe an extra long time of silence – perhaps quarter of an hour – in which to sit quietly or take a walk.

Music
Listen to a piece of tranquil music on the theme of quietness, perhaps a hymn like 'I lift my eyes to the quiet hills' by Timothy

Dudley-Smith, or 'Be still, for the presence of the Lord' by David Evans; or perhaps something reflective like Schumann's 'Träumerei' or Gluck's 'Dance of the Blessed Spirits'.

Silence

Reflective prayer: The comma
Who'd have thought it –
   something as small as a comma
   making such a difference?
But it did,
   the sentence making little sense without it.
It indicated a pause for breath,
   small but vital;
   that little break key to the whole.

Remind me, Lord, that *I* need to pause sometimes
   if I'm to make sense of life,
   time to stop and stare essential if I'm to keep things in balance
   and live as you intend.
In the many demands and duties I face each day,
   teach me to make space for stillness and quiet –
   space for me and you.
Amen.

Silence

Meditation
It was the simplest of sounds,
   the song of a skylark high in the sky,
   but to me, Lord, that day it was the song of an angel,
   a harbinger of peace.

I stood and listened spellbound,
   transported to another world,
   for in that joyful music,
   those innocent notes,
   there came back memories of carefree days
   and tranquil moments,
   of life untouched by the endless quest for gain.
And I rejoiced, Lord, in the beauty of it all,
   savouring the magic of that moment –
   my thoughts still,
   my mind calm,
   my soul at rest.
I realised then how I needed that moment,
   for I'd lost sight of self,
   of life,
   of you –
   but suddenly I saw again,
   the nagging fears and hidden doubts,
   the crowding concerns and frantic haste,
   all put into perspective beside the things that really count,
   and I wanted simply to stay, Lord,
   lest the spell be broken
   and peace be lost.

My child,
   you *did* need that time, just as you say,
   those quiet few moments to hear again my still small voice,
   but if you were afraid to let go in case you lost me,
   scared to move on in case you fell back,
   then you either didn't get the message
   or failed to hear it all.
For the peace I offer is not just a fleeting thing,
   here today and gone tomorrow;
   it's an inner serenity that will not be shaken,
   a calmness of spirit in the fiercest of storms.

Don't try to make sense of it, for it's beyond expression,
    unlike anything the world can give;
    for even in the most troubled of moments
    and hectic of days,
    you will find stillness of mind and rest for your soul.
So come to me now, and let my love enfold you,
    then turn around and go in peace.

Silence

Reflective prayer: The holiday

I needed that break, more than I realised,
    for in the bustle of each day
    I'd lost touch with the simple but special things in life.
I had time, suddenly, to stop, stare, pause and ponder –
    to appreciate flowers in bloom and birds in song,
    the scent of the sea and caress of the breeze,
    uplifting the heart and soothing the spirit,
    gifts beyond price.
Teach me, Lord, whatever else needs doing,
    to make time to unwind and hear your voice,
    to be still and glimpse your presence.
Save me from being so concerned with the daily demands of life
    that I have no time left truly to live.
Amen.

Silence

Reflective prayer: The switch

I left it switched on,
    even though I was going away,
    and when I returned a few days later

it was to find the batteries flat,
    drained of all power,
    no good for anything until they had been fully recharged.

I forget that I too, Lord, need to switch off sometimes,
    if I'm not to end up exhausted.
Teach me to appreciate the importance of being still,
    of taking a breather from the demands of life,
    however pressing they may be.
Show me the difference between doing enough
    and doing too much,
    and help me to get the balance right.
Amen.

Silence

Meditation

I'll never forget it, Lord,
    that moment as I stood on the hilltop
    and took in the sight before me –
    the sun golden on the horizon,
    the sea stretching out into the distance, blue as topaz,
    the cliffs white as snow,
    and the seagulls soaring overhead in lofty splendour.
It was magnificent,
    a taste of paradise,
    the world as I'd never seen it before,
    full of beauty and wonder.
I heard cows lowing and sheep calling their young,
    birds singing in the distance and bees droning among the heather,
    the laughter of the waves
    and the playful whispering of grass stirred by the breeze,
    each joining to create a jubilant chorus,

an outpouring of celebration,
    a hymn of praise.
And my heart joined in the dance,
    leaping with delight,
    skipping with pleasure,
    crying out in adoration.
For here was freedom and inexpressible loveliness,
    life as it ought to be,
    creation in all its glory.
It was wonderful, Lord,
    a glimpse of your majesty,
    a revelation of your handiwork,
    a sign of your love –
    and in that moment, as never before, I gave you my worship.

My child,
    this may come as a surprise,
    but that moment was precious to me as well as you,
    for the wonder in your eyes and the joy in your face
    was a prayer greater than all words,
    an expression of gratitude I shall always treasure.
So thank you for your worship,
    and thank you for taking time to stop and stare,
    to glimpse my presence in the beauty of creation,
    to reflect on my handiwork and know me by your side.
Don't lose that sense of awe,
    for it is a gateway to heaven,
    a foretaste of my eternal kingdom.
Yet remember also there is more to discover –
    that if you found me once in a moment of quietness,
    you must find me always in every place and every moment.
Make time to withdraw, of course,
    but then return,
    back to the daily round of life.
Make time to pause,

but then resume,
    picking up where you left off.
Make time to reflect,
    but then to act,
    seeing my presence in the place where I have placed you,
    for when you have learned that, my child,
    we shall dance together for all eternity.

Silence

Prayer

O great Spirit,
    teach me to think quietly,
    to speak gently
    and to hear thy voice in the whispering breeze,
    the song of birds
    and in the murmuring brook.
Amen.

Anon

Silence

Poem: Evensong

Here beneath the evening sun,
I stand alone, and rest, at one
with all that in the tranquil air
inspires me to stop and stare.
The day's confusion left behind
as in the solitude I find
a quiet deep and undisturbed
by troubles of this fleeting world.

71

Life's frantic fever fades until
my mind is calm and soul is still –
such moments able to impart
a special peace within my heart.

Silence

Reflective prayer
I looked for peace, Lord,
   but I didn't find it.
I looked at the world,
   but saw there division and discord –
   person divided against person
   and nation against nation;
   hatred, greed and bitterness breeding violence and war.
I looked at myself,
   but saw there a restless striving after contentment,
   an outward calm masking an inner turmoil.
I looked at the Church,
   and even there the wounds ran deep –
   conflict over worship and doctrine,
   clashes of temperament and personality,
   petty disputes dividing Christian from Christian,
   fellowship from fellowship,
   estranging us from you and one another.
I looked for peace, Lord,
   but didn't find it until I looked to you,
   and then I found rest for my soul,
   a haven from the storm,
   a quietness deep within.
Amen.

Silence

Proverbs and sayings

- How can you expect God to speak in that gentle and inward voice which melts the soul, when you are making so much noise with your rapid reflections? Be silent, and God will speak again. (François Fenelon)

- God is a tranquil Being, and abides in a tranquil eternity. So must thy spirit become a tranquil and clear little pool, wherein the serene light of God can be mirrored. (Gerhard Tersteegen)

- To go up alone into the mountain and come back as an ambassador to the world, has ever been the method of humanity's best friends. (Evelyn Underhill)

- All the troubles of humankind come upon us because we cannot sit quietly in a room. (Blaise Pascal)

- If we do not have quiet in our minds, outward comfort will do no more for us than a golden slipper on a gouty foot. (John Bunyan)

- Practise the art of 'aloneness' and you will discover the treasure of tranquillity. Develop the art of solitude and you will unearth the gift of serenity. (William W. Ward)

- The very best and utmost attainment in this life is to remain still and let God act and speak in thee. (Meister Eckhart)

- Life is not measured by the number of breaths we take, but by the moments that take our breath away. (Anon)

- Always remember to slow down in life; live, breathe and learn; take a look around you whenever you have time, and never forget everything and every person that has the least place within your heart. (Anon)

- Quiet minds cannot be perplexed or frightened but go on in fortune or misfortune at their own private pace, like a clock during a thunderstorm. (Robert Louis Stevenson)

- Sit in reverie and watch the changing colour of the waves that break upon the idle seashore of the mind. (Henry Wadsworth Longfellow)

- God is the friend of silence. See how nature – trees, flowers, grass – grows in silence; see the stars, the moon and the sun, how they move in silence . . . We need silence to be able to touch souls. (Mother Teresa)

Silence

Closing prayer

O God, you are the unsearchable abyss of peace,
    the ineffable sea of love,
    and the fountain of blessings.
Water us with plenteous streams,
    from the riches of your grace;
    and from the most sweet springs of your kindness,
    make us children of quietness and heirs of peace.
Amen.

Clement of Alexandria (c. 150–c. 215)